home.

home.

Bakhtawar Mehdi

home.

Copyright © 2020 Bakhtawar Mehdi
All rights reserved. Printed in the United States of America. No part of this publication may be used or reproduced in any manner whatsoever without written permission of the author except in the case of reprints in the context of reviews.

MG Media

Design by Maria Azhar

ISBN: 978-0-5787-1047-1

Library of Congress Control Number: 2020910571

To the unwavering light
of my own true self,
who continually guides me
on the journey home,
illuminating the path
through shadows,
and nurturing
the courage to be.

contents

the season of noise ………………....……… 11

the season of silence ……………………….. 41

the season of beauty ………………………. 71

muradan magne walay kam na honge
dene wala karam karta rahega

Seekers will never cease to ask for
their desires, and the Giver will never
cease to shower His grace

the season of noise

home.

storms raged within me

bakhtawar mehdi

Eyes full
of questions
and wonder
a stranger
reflected back
who had I become

home.

Was this it
was this *all*
then why
did I still
feel my heart
calling to
the one
I could not
name

bakhtawar mehdi

The dark sky
whispered
me awake
many nights
too afraid
to see
I drowned
in the depths
of sleep

home.

There is a
humming
silence
in the noise

bakhtawar mehdi

It is never strangers
who crack our hearts
break our spirits
in the name of
anything

home.

A twinkle in the eyes
as they watched
rivers of pain
flow from my soul

  - *crazy*

Be strong
they said
as I was
plucked
from the garden
and thrown
into a volcano

home.

Rooted
in blood
but not
in soul

The nights
grew longer
as I suffocated
in a strange land
that was no longer
mine

home.

Let the noise
reach the
highest skies
it will
not silence
the echoes
of your
heart

bakhtawar mehdi

why are you afraid to *think*

home.

Is it stillness you fear
or the illusions
of silence
it will disrupt

bakhtawar mehdi

Let the tongues
sing as they may
listen to the eyes
for dishonest tales

home.

Silly *you*
how will
you survive
when you have
paper to burn
but no heart
to keep alive

   - love is everything

As I looked out
into the night sky
I only wished to
evaporate into the
cool breeze

home.

An earth I had
always
thought of
vast
shrunk
as I began to see
far galaxies

bakhtawar mehdi

They fear for
you to see your own
breathtaking being
in all its light

home.

you are…
you are…
you are…

   - *I am*

I whispered
to the moon
telling her
all the desires
I would keep
hidden from
the sun

home.

Do not fear the shadows
they hide within them
the peace your heart seeks

Embrace
this season
with its tears
laughter
and truths
for there is
always
a purpose

home.

Darkness is a gift
it illuminates the light
that is *you*

bakhtawar mehdi

Always a fighter
twirling
through the pain
to the sound of
breaking glass
and growing
thorns

home.

The words
stopped
flowing
from the veins
of my heart
and then I knew

   - *all things come and go*

bakhtawar mehdi

I savored
the last few
bitter breaths
for I knew
it was time

home.

I choose me

the season of silence

home.

be brave my heart
you are home

I no longer cared
to be understood
by anyone
but my own
being

home.

The worse has passed
do not be afraid now
to look at the wound

You have always
made magic
out of the tragic

home.

Fed beasts
pieces of
your own
flesh

bakhtawar mehdi

Birthed life
from destruction

home.

Crumbs will never fill
a starving heart
you will always yearn
for more

Listen to the words
that are not spoken
but felt

home.

see
so
you may
see
what you
cannot
see

bakhtawar mehdi

History repeats
with burning flesh
and choking tears

home.

Do not be blind
to the ugliness
of evils
that surround you

  - *speak*

bakhtawar mehdi

Cry my son
cry
do not go
through a lifetime
with a weeping
soul

home.

Rip off
the masks
of cruelty
that hide
your fears

The self
will knock
and if you
do not answer
it will shatter
all walls
that stand
between

home.

Bring out
which is
within you
and let it
guide you

bakhtawar mehdi

Do the hearts
tremble
of the takers
when they reach
to touch
that which they
cannot savor

home.

the hearts speak

bakhtawar mehdi

You must understand
the smaller pieces
the darker pieces
the forgotten pieces

  - *wholeness*

home.

I am
not the soil
that formed me
not the language
that flows from
my tongue
not the body
I call home
they flow
through me
yet
I am only
me

In silence
you can see
the fleeting
moments
of this
strange
world

home.

All seasons
come and go

Allow air to flow through
shine light through the cracks
wrap it with love

- to heal a wound

home.

To be free
is to feel
the fear
in each
moment
as a visitor
that comes
and goes

One day
you will see the pain
flow out of you

- *sweet goodbyes*

home.

Chasing shadows
only to be brought back
to the mirror
of my own soul

The sun melted
into my skin
as the breeze
laid a kiss
the taste of
sweet freedom
in the air

- walk to the mailbox

home.

I am unbecoming
to become
me

the season of beauty

home.

you
are
your
home
love
nurture
and
protect

bakhtawar mehdi

I have been
a wanderer
all my life
heart always
in search
of a lingering scent
I could not see

home.

Lifetimes spent
chasing that which
had never left
my *own* being

bakhtawar mehdi

From sunrise
to sunset
I vow to answer
every passionate call
of my soul

home.

Step out of the desert
and you will find
oceans of rubies
awaiting you

bakhtawar mehdi

I fell so madly in love
with the depths of the night
too afraid to miss a dancing star
I could never fall asleep again

home.

Once you can *see*
you will know of
nothing else

Make peace
with the
whispering noise
and humming silence

  - walk in beauty

home.

All that stood
between
everything and me
was always
only
me

Growing
is a slow dance
keep moving
for as long as
the universe
gifts you
another song

home.

Open your heart
to your love
to your light
to your beauty
to you

bakhtawar mehdi

Stand in your truth
and do not bend
to the winds of illusion
that may befall

home.

fall
get up
fall
get up
fall
get up

   - always *get up*

bakhtawar mehdi

The universe
says
sing
dance
shout
put it out there
in any way
and
I will
answer

home.

A breeze of change
arrives each morning

bakhtawar mehdi

Lay
under the
night sky
and count
the blessings
of stardust
that are
showered
upon you

home.

Rivers of honey
sing out
for your heart

bakhtawar mehdi

I could explore
the galaxies within me
for a lifetime
and then some

home.

Beauty is felt
through the heart

Make a wish
hide it within
your heart
it is yours

   - *promise*

home.

In peace
there is power
In beauty
there is power
In you
there is power

bakhtawar mehdi

You are the son
of a dreamer
the daughter
of a warrior
they bled
for the wings
that let you
soar

home.

you are love
you are beauty
you are home

You are everything
and nothing
majestics of the world
and a speckle
of dust

  - *flowing*

home.

You are closer to me
than the being
of my own soul

All the words
they are from you
and for you

  - *infinite bounties*

home.

From the earth
I was raised
to the earth
I will be laid
and here
in between
the seasons of
my life
I embrace

BAKHTAWAR MEHDI

Born in Pakistan and breathing in the United States, Bakhtawar Mehdi finds 'home' in the luminous moments connecting her two worlds and her journey within. With insights from her background in Psychology and as the founder of The Wellness Quest—a platform dedicated to holistic well-being and authentic self-discovery- *home* is her debut poetry collection.

www.thewellnessquest.co

www.ingramcontent.com/pod-product-compliance
Lightning Source LLC
Chambersburg PA
CBHW061335040426
42444CB00011B/2926